Sports Training Business Guide

Forward:

I use examples in this manual from my basketball skills training business, but the concepts (finding a place for your training, what to say to parents and players, how to structure lessons, etc.) are adaptable for any sports training business.

If you have any questions, just send me an email at:
sportscoachbiz@gmail.com

Bill Dale

Copyright Notice:

Authored/Published by:

Bill Dale
Phone/Text: 302-751-0045
Email: sportscoachbiz@gmail.com

Printed in the United States of America

Disclaimer and Legal Notices:

Table of Contents

Congratulations!

First, I want to say…Thanks for investing in this material.

If you truly love to teach sports, this will be one of the greatest investments you've ever made.

This all started from my desire to teach kids how to become better players in the sport that I coached - basketball. And it comes from my first-hand experience of seeing how much this type of thing (teaching sports) is wanted in communities all over the world.

Now I can help even more kids to become better athletes by helping you to become a much **needed** (and much **_wanted_**) sports skills development coach.

You Are Needed *And* Wanted…

I say "needed", because you and I both know that there is a great need for coaches who can take the time to teach kids all the necessary skills it takes to play various sports. Team coaches today have very little time to develop each player on their team.

Depending on the sport, there's just not enough time to develop team strategies, go over offensive and defensive schemes, and focus for the next games, *plus* give individualized attention to every single player on the team.

That's why it's important to have someone who can take players who want to develop some part (or parts) of their game, and show them the necessary steps to improvement.

That someone is <u>you</u>.

I say "wanted", because like I said earlier, I have seen how much parents and players want this service.

And I know there are many, many more who want this. (For my basketball lessons business, I got emails from all over the United States as well as from parts of Africa and Australia and England from parents who wanted to enroll their kids in lessons and wanted help finding a private coach.)

1

But these types of emails and my experiences in my business prove that **parents and players are very eager to get guidance from someone who can help them develop their skills**. They want someone who can give them guidance in becoming a better athlete. And they will pay someone to do it.

That someone is <u>you</u>.

It's Not Just About "Winning", Or Even About The Sport Itself…

A little warning – you might hear or read things in the paper from parents or "child welfare" type organizations who talk about "pushing kids too far" or "putting too much pressure on kids to win".

There are certain parents and instructors who fit this description. Just go to any little league game and you'll see it – parents and coaches screaming at players and sometimes at each other. But that's not what this is about.

Like I said, I starting doing this because I wanted to help kids get better at a game they love. I also like the idea of teaching kids to have goals and to overcome obstacles (not only in sports, but maybe in life, too).

Never once in my lessons with players or my conversations with parents have I said anything about winning more games or anything like that.

What I do talk about when I first start working with a player is that I will help them to develop fundamental skills, as well as work with them to achieve certain goals they have in terms of the lessons (for basketball, this means becoming a better free throw shooter, getting good at dribbling, etc.).

As an example, in my basketball lessons, I worked with a young girl who had problems with layups. After only 20 minutes, I had her doing layups smoothly.

I stopped her and said to her: "I just saw you go from not being able to shoot layups on either side, to being able to do them on <u>both</u> sides (using her left hand *and* her right hand) with ease. Now you know that you can get better at just about anything if you practice and work at it."

Now, hopefully for the rest of her life, she realizes that if she has problems with something, or she comes across a tough situation (not just in basketball), she knows that she can work her way through it, even if it takes awhile. That's one of the many mindsets I like to stress with the players I work with. It's not <u>*just*</u> about basketball (or whatever sport they might play).

If a player I'm working with is already skillful, and is already a "good" player, I can give them certain skills that will help them to the next level or give them an extra edge if they come up against a

2

player of equal skill. For them, it's more about how they approach the game and how they think about the game.

Other times, working with free throw shooters who are already good, I explain to them how I will help them get that "in the zone" stroke, and stay there (in the zone) longer.

What I'm doing with all the players I work with is showing them that there's a way to build a disciplined approach to improvement that goes beyond basketball. It involves their mindset and attitude too.

So it's a special kind of attitude you need to focus on with this business and the sport you teach. Don't listen to all those whiners about pushing kids too hard. Remember, the parents and players who come to you want to be there.

(*If you do come across a player who you think doesn't want to be there with you, but the parents insist, then it's your responsibility to tell the parents that you will not do the lessons because you feel that their child doesn't want to be there. I have to say though, that I've never run into this kind of situation with my business.*).

All the kids will love it, if you make it interesting for them.

A Brief Background:
How I Got Started…

Back in 2002, I heard about a guy doing private baseball pitching lessons in the western U.S. I got some information from him and saw what he was doing. I immediately knew that I wanted to do this for basketball.

I've always liked the idea of helping kids play better basketball, but I realized that I wasn't the type to coach a team. It takes a special kind of person to take a bunch of kids and mold them into a good team. If that is you, great. I admire you.

But I get greater satisfaction by working with one player (or a couple players) at a time, finding out what they need help with, and then working with them to help them develop their skills.

So, when I discovered that other coaches were doing this, I thought to myself: "You can get paid for teaching kids how to play basketball." There really was no decision to it. It was a no-brainer. I instantly went to work putting together my plans for this business, from what I would teach, to how to market this service to parents and players.

And you can do this too, with the sport that you coach. I'll show you how to get started.

3

Finding A Place For Your Lessons…

The only real snag I came across was where to do the lessons. And this will probably be the hardest part about getting started for you.

For my basketball lessons, I had problems finding a school that would let me use a gym. All the public schools were dead ends. I don't know about your area, but in mine, I think they are kind of "backward" in their thinking. I won't go into detail here, but they wouldn't even give me a chance.

It took me over 3 months to find a gym. So let me give you advice based on my experience: try to find a private school who will rent you the gym or let you use space (a field) on their property.

Find out what it costs to rent the gym. Then try to make a deal with the head of the school or athletic director where you'll give discounts to the players at their school if you can use the gym for discounted rental fees. You'll have to decide what you can pay and what you can charge for your services in your area, so make sure the numbers work out for you.

I've never had to do this, but if forced to, I would have used an outdoor court for my basketball training. It's nice to have an indoor court because then you don't have to worry about canceling lessons if there is bad weather. But if forced to, I would have used an outdoor court. I know several coaches who do that for their lessons.

If you coach a sport that you don't need a gym for, that's even better. You can usually use a school's field (if their team isn't using it - just get permission) or find a park area with some space. For example, if you teach baseball pitching, you can get a pitching mound rubber, a home plate, and a backstop net and go to a park with open space.

Another option is to find a local YMCA or athletic club that has space and time slots for you to rent. If you have to go this route, then approach the facility manager about setting up skills clinics for players. You'll be more likely to get to rent the facilities if you explain how it will benefit their members or explain to them that you'll be bringing money in for them.

One-on-One Training
Or Small Groups…

I like to work with one player at a time so I can focus on the needs of that player. Sometimes I will work with 2 or 3 players (but no more than that), and I just adapt my individual drills for those 2-or-3-player groups.

Once again, if you coach a sport that needs a gym, and you can only find one that charges a lot for you to use the court, you might have to do small groups (3 to 5 players, or more if you have somebody helping you) so you can make enough money to pay the rent and to keep some for yourself.

4

Setting Fees…

Let me say again that parents and players <u>want</u> this service. Parents know that you are giving them a valuable service of individualized instruction for their kid(s), and the players know that they can't get this kind of attention from just any coach.

So, the only convincing that you'll have to do about your fees is convincing yourself to set your fees as high as possible. Charge as much as you can for your area. I've heard of other training coaches who charge upwards of $75 – $125 per hour. But it can be anywhere from $30 on up.

With that said, a lot of your decision about fees will have to do with where you do your lessons. If you find a small gym that charges you a lot of money to use the facilities, then you will have to charge your students a high enough fee so you can make money.

If you coach a sport that doesn't need a gym, you can find an open area to do the lessons and just about all of your fee will be profit.

One thing to consider...If you have a hard time finding a gym or place to do your lessons, you can approach a school (a private school) to make a deal. You can let them know you'll charge less for their students. It's a win-win for both you and the school. You get to use the facilities and they (their students) get discounted rates. Just do what works for you.

Setting Up Your Business…

I want to say again that I'm not an attorney and I don't give legal or accounting advice. So the following is a general guideline for setting up your business.

You need to check with your state to find out what you need to do to start a business. An easy way to find out is to go to www.google.com and type in your state and the words "starting a business" or "business forms".

For example, type in "Maryland" and "business forms". In the search results is the link to Maryland's state government's website. There you can find info on starting a business as well as links to other sites that are helpful with business issues.

Anyway, you'll find out what you need to do to get going as well as how to get set up to pay taxes on the money you bring in from your business. You also need to check for any other requirements for doing business in your state.

And you need to check with your local government to see if you need to do anything special. Call your county courthouse or local chamber of commerce and ask them about requirements for starting and running a business in your specific area.

Insurance / Liability Issues…

With yet another reminder that I'm not an attorney and I don't give legal advice, this is what I've done in my situation…

I've used a Liability Release Form that covers the conceivable injury scenarios. I've never had a parent who wouldn't sign this. I just explain to them that the gym I'm using requires me to have some sort of protection. (Contact a local attorney or an online legal source if you want to find out more about a liability release.)

Here's the deal. Most parents know what kinds of risks are involved with sports. What you have to watch out for is any kind of horseplay on breaks when you are doing small groups. If you just do single-player lessons, this isn't an issue. And even in the small group setting, the kids who are coming to the lessons are there to learn and are usually not the type to fool around.

As far as getting insurance, just do a search on Google for "liability insurance private sports coach" or something similar. There are companies who offer policies. Here are a couple links that I've come across:

SadlerSports.com

Nationwide.com

Online coaching database CoachUp.com includes liability coverage for the coaches in their database. (More about CoachUp on the next page.)

I haven't worked with either of these companies. I'm putting links here so you can take a look to see what is involved. Do some research and find the best one for you and your situation. If you are already a coach that is employed at a school, see if you can be covered by their insurance or if there is something you need to do to be covered.

With all that said, I've never had anything go wrong in the couple of years that I've taught lessons. I've had one boy sprain his ankle, and I just gave him an ice-pack. (By the way, his injury happened about ten minutes into his lesson. I didn't charge his father for the lesson. I think that's just common decency to do that in that situation).

6

I think it's a good idea to have CPR and First Aid training. If something should happen, it's good to know how to take control of the situation. Plus, these things are good to know even if you aren't going to coach. You never know when you might need to use those skills.

Another thing that I've come across is parents dropping off their kid(s) for the lessons and then coming back to pick them up at the end of the hour. I've never had a problem with that. The longer you do this, the more you get to know the parents and players, but you never really can be 100% sure that you'll never be accused of something.

One idea to cover yourself is to have a video camera record your sessions in their entirety. Just set the camera in a corner so it captures everything for the entire hour. That way you have physical evidence. Like I said, I've never had a problem with something serious like this, but you have to decide for yourself what you want to do if you have parents drop their kids off for lessons.

Getting Customers

I will show you some samples of my marketing materials in the next section, starting on pg. 14. But here are a few of the things you should do first.

CoachUp.com

First, go to CoachUp.com. It is an online database of coaches for customers to search for private sports lessons in their area.

This is taken directly from CoachUp.com:

Connect with clients to grow your coaching business

CoachUp provides marketing tools to reach new clients outside your word-of-mouth network and grow your coaching business.

CoachUp handles everything - just show up and coach

Client management tools to message your clients, receive client payments directly in your bank account, and manage your schedule. Manage your business on the go with our convenient mobile app.

CoachUp protects you

$1,000,000 in liability insurance coverage for all sessions booked through CoachUp and our Customer Care team is here to help you at anytime.

(*NOTE: I am in no way affiliated with CoachUp, nor do I receive any compensation for mentioning CoachUp.)

As great a service as CoachUp is, there are other ways that you should market your sports lessons business.

Facebook Page

It's also a good idea to have a Facebook page for your business.

It's a good idea to update it regularly with posts about any training issues that you have in your sport, as well as videos of some of your training sessions so potential customers can see you in action. (Just get permission from parents before posting any pictures or videos of their kids.)

Just remember to include all your contact info on your page so it comes up when people do Facebook or Google searches for local lessons.

Your Own Website

Having your own website is great for sharing all of your information about your business. This includes all of the contact info and info about lessons, but also for posting pictures, videos, and blog posts.

There are several good options for doing this. You can use simple website builders like SquareSpace, Wix, and Weebly. They all have templates that are simple to use for all your webpages, videos, and blog posts.

Just like with your Facebook page, it's a good idea to update it regularly with posts about any training issues that you have in your sport, as well as videos of some of your training sessions so potential customers can see you in action. (Again, get permission from parents before posting any pictures or videos of their kids.)

Host any videos you make on Youtube and then embed them into your website (easy to do with those website builders I just talked about).

Having your own website is also great for showing up in search results in Google when someone is looking for coaches who offer lessons in your area.

Word Of Mouth

The absolute best way to get a new customer is through word-of-mouth referrals. Whatever someone else says about you is 100 times more powerful than what you can say about yourself in an ad or on a website.

Think about this for a minute…Jimmy signs up for lessons with you and after a few weeks his performance has improved so much that his father can't help but brag about it. Plus, if it's during the season, everyone else will notice how much Jimmy has improved, so people will be talking to his parents. And when the parents say, "Oh he's been working with so-and-so…", that's more valuable for you than anything you can say about yourself on your website or on a flyer.

A great way to get these kinds of referrals, and a great way to fill up your schedule with very little effort, is if you can get in good with one or two schools. When I found a private school that let me rent their gym, I had a built-in customer base. After I got one or two players from that school to sign up for lessons, more and more just seemed to fall right in place.

Stimulating referrals and word of mouth:

You can cause your customers to refer other parents and players to you by:

    1 - Asking them to do it (let them know that you like them to refer others);

    2 – Rewarding them with gifts when they do it and when someone signs up;

    3 – Rewarding the new customer when they sign up through a referral.

So, a couple of weeks after Mrs. Johnson signs up with you (after her son has gone through a few lessons, and she can see how much you are helping him), you talk to Mrs. Johnson and let her know that you like working with her son and that you like working with other kids who are like him. You then give her some of your flyers (examples of those later), so that she can pass them out to other parents she knows who might be interested.

Then, one day Mrs. Johnson talks to Mr. Smith and tells him about you and how you have helped her son with his free throws (if you are doing basketball, for example) and she gives him a flyer. Mr. Smith contacts you and then signs his daughter up for lessons.

Let me tell you, if you are doing everything else right with your lessons, then you can get this kind of referral machine going and can get it to feed you customers just about forever. Then you can get to the point where you have to turn people away because you are using all the available time slots that you have.

It's a good place to be in with your business. When you are booked solid, people know that you are in demand. Then you can raise your fees! And you can get to this point if you can put a referral system like this in place.

When You First Talk To Parents or Players

My goal is to try to sign the players up for a set of ongoing lessons right off the bat. If you are sure that you can get the gym or field or practice area for regularly scheduled times, you'll want to do the same.

First of all, players need to be consistent when learning new skills, so multiple lessons need to happen.

Also, try to get paid up front for however many weeks are in your package of lessons that you offer. Then when those are finished, you can sign them up for another set of weekly lessons. Do it in chunks so you can get more money up front.

And it helps you plan your schedule better, instead just scheduling just one lesson over and over, let them know that it's better to commit to a package of several lessons over a few weeks. This shouldn't be a problem. Most of them have already committed to becoming better (that's why they are coming to you), so it shouldn't be hard to convince them.

You might have some parents and players who will only want to pay week-by-week. This is because they might have other commitments and can't be there for consecutive weeks, or whatever. That's o.k. when you have the openings to do that. If your scheduling allows it, why not.

(Just make sure that they let you know as soon as they can when they are not going to be there for any particular week, so that you can plan accordingly. It's not fun getting to the gym or field ready to do a lesson and no one shows up. Make it known up front that that kind of thing is unacceptable. I've never had a real bad problem with this, and I don't want you to go through it.)

When someone new first calls or contacts you, and for some reason they don't want to commit to signing up for a package of lessons, ask them if they want to sign up for just one lesson. They can get a feeling of what you do by coming to that first lesson without having to commit to a lot of sessions.

Usually that's all it takes, but if for some reason the parent still doesn't want to commit to signing up for lessons or to even come in for a one-time lesson, you can offer them one <u>free</u> lesson so they can "try me out" if you have the time slot available for it. I only had to do this maybe once or twice. And I would do it every time if I had to.

Why would I do that?…every parent who calls or emails you asking about training will potentially give you hundreds of dollars a year (and be worth much more in referrals) throughout their lifetime as your customer. So if you have the time slot available, it wouldn't be that bad to give up that first hour for free to show them how good the lessons will be for their child.

And when they come in for their first workout, they can talk to the other parents who are there waiting for their kid to get finished with their lesson. That's why it would be good to schedule a new player where his or her first lesson is after another player who's been with you for awhile.

They'll usually get there early and they can see what you're doing with the other player(s) and they can get some idea from just watching.

Anyway, in almost every case, the parent(s) will be "pre-sold" on doing the lessons. They want the best for their kid(s), so they are willing to pay to sign up for individualized training. So really, all you have to do is agree on a time (where you can fit them into your schedule).

Thank You Gifts

Like I said, I like to give gifts when I get a parent to sign up their kid. This is because I really am thankful for them to give me a chance to work with their son or daughter.

You can give any kind of gift as a "sign-up Thank You". I've used gift certificates to sporting goods stores and restaurants. But it can be anything.

The Crown Trophy company (*CrownTrophy.com*) also has pins you can use as gifts for people who sign up with you.

Other Customer Issues:

"Do you have references?"

Sometimes when a parent calls or emails me for information on lessons, they'll ask me for references. I don't give out names and addresses of other parents and students I work with because I'm big on privacy and I don't want to bother them (even though most of them would gladly do it for me).

I don't blame parents for asking this. They just want to make sure they are getting good advice and instruction for their children. What you can do is invite them to watch one of your lessons so they can see what happens.

If your new customers come from referrals, you don't have to go through these kinds of explanations (which is why you want to have your referral system in place as soon as you can). But when you are starting out, you might be asked this kind of question.

If you do have someone who doesn't mind being called and you can use them for a reference, then go ahead. It can only help you. If not, then you can always offer this new potential customer the "free lesson / try-me-out deal" that I talked about on pg. 10 as a last resort to prove you know what you are doing.

But that should only be necessary when you're just starting out. Once you get a lot of clients, your slots/times for new customers will be mostly filled, which should prove to them that you know what you're doing.

"Can you make my kid a starter?"

I once had a parent ask me if I could make his daughter a starter on her AAU basketball squad. I told him that I could make her a better player, but I couldn't guarantee that she'd become a starter for her team.

First of all, since I didn't know her, I didn't know what her practice habits were. Sure she was a talented player, but just because a player has talent doesn't mean they are a hard worker.

It's all up to the individual player to use what you give them. You can show them everything you know, but if they go home and do nothing for the entire week until their next lesson, then they are not taking advantage of your knowledge. They need to practice what you show them.

Plus, I didn't know who her AAU coach was. A lot of coaches have their set rotation and favorite players, so no matter how much someone might improve, if the coach has favorites on his team, then there's nothing you can do about it.

So, there are all kinds of factors that prevent you from guaranteeing anything like that. If coaching were that easy, we'd all be able to win high school state championships or go to the NCAA Final Four every year.

One Last Thing

In the past several years, the state of the economy (especially in the U.S.) has been in the news almost every day.

I want to tell you that you should **not** let that influence how you go about this business. You should **not** let the "bad economy" (or the perceived "bad economy") stop you or cause you to think you won't be able to be successful.

12

There are many examples of businesses who have thrived in so called "bad economies". One example that comes to mind is an insurance company that was started in the Great Depression of the last century (1930's), which was far worse than anything we have gone through the past several years.

Anyway, that company was started by a man named W. Clement Stone, and he became a millionaire in that "bad economy." I tell you this just to show you an example (one of many I could give you) that outside influences canNOT totally control your success.

Another way to say it, is...**Your success has more to do with how you think than how others think.** *(That's also the attitude you need to show and transfer to your students and players).*

Plus, you should know that one of the things that parents don't stop spending money for is their kids, especially if gives them skills that will help them.

As long as you show parents that you'll help their kids develop skills, and as long as you can find these parents and players, you should succeed.

13

How To Get Customers

Students of the School Where you do lessons:

If you are able to use a school's facilities for your training, you have a built-in group of customers. Like I said back on pgs. 4 and 5, you can offer the head of the school and the coaches there to do training for their students at a discount. This might be all you need to fill up your schedule, and it can happen quickly if there are a lot of students there who want individual training.

One problem (but a good one to have) is if more students than you have time for individually want training. Then you might have to do group sessions. Just try to keep groups in manageable numbers. You might even need to have an assistant with you so each player gets attention.

Website:

On the pg. 19 is a copy of my first website. The technology has become so much better and it is so much easier now to put up a site to show off what you can teach. As I said earlier, you can go to Squarespace, Wix, or Weebly to subscribe to a monthly website host plan. All the tools you need are on each of those platforms.

You should also create a **Facebook Page** for your business. You can do that through your personal account. It's very simple.

Anyway, on my site, I gave them an overall description of what the lessons are all about. (I call my lessons "Training" because sometimes kids, especially boys, don't like the idea of having to take "lessons". They want to see themselves as working with a trainer instead).

I describe who I work with (beginners, players with some experience, and experienced players). This is to let parents know that I can work with players at all levels, and can customize lessons for them.

Then I ask for their contact info. I want this for a number of reasons:

> 1) A lot will probably email you first. Some will call, and that is easier to start the whole process, but a lot might email you first for more info.
>
> 2) So I can send them information that explains what I do (about how I work as well as go over training information that is on the website and in the flyers - see pgs. 21 and 22 for the flyers)
>
> 3) To set up the process so the parent is coming to me for advice (instead of me going out and "cold calling" parents to see if they are interested in getting lessons for their kids). Someone who comes to you looking for help because you are an "expert" is much more

likely to buy what you have than someone who is approached by you when you are just trying to sell them something.

4) So I can contact them again and make them a "Try Me Out" Offer (like I talked about at the bottom of pg. 10) if they don't sign up for a package of lessons.

5) I like to send gifts (gift certificates, Thanksgiving and Christmas cards, etc.) later on after I have worked with their kid. You want to treat your customers like gold, because they are choosing to give you their money and time. And by the way, when was the last time you got a good gift from a business you use a lot? It doesn't happen that often does it? So just imagine how much you'll stick out when you send gifts to your customers.

You don't have to ask for their physical address. I did it at that time so I could send them info in the mail. Now all you really need is a phone # and email. You can get their address for mailing them stuff later after they get to know you.

Near the end, I tell them that I only have a set number of spots available (which is the truth), so there is urgency to contact me as soon as possible if they are even the slightest bit interested.

At the end, there is a quote from the athletic director of the school where I did the lessons. This is to give a little more credibility and is more believable than anything I can say about myself. Whenever you get somebody talking good about you, ask them if you can use what they say to help you get more customers.

This is called "word of mouth" and it's probably the most powerful thing you can use to get new customers. People trust what other people say about you more than what you say about you.

One-on-One Basketball Training

Focusing on Shooting, Passing, Dribbling, Offensive Moves, and the "Mental Game"

Helps develop higher levels of Accuracy, Consistency, and Concentration...
and leads to more Confidence, Assertiveness, and more Fun

From: Bill Dale
Elkton, Md

Dear parent or coach,

If you have a son, daughter, or player who would like to improve their game, I've put together special basketball training programs for players of all ages and skill levels.

These private one-on-one training sessions are for:

- **beginners** who want help with the fundamentals,
- **players who have some experience** and are looking to get to the next level,
- and **experienced players** who want that extra "edge" over the competition.

Each player gets customized training to fit their game (all players are different, so the training will be "made to fit" each player). And a big part of the training and skill development is done through video analysis - I use a digital video camera (with slow motion playback) during drills for immediate feedback. Players learn much faster if they can **see for themselves** what they are doing right and what they are doing wrong.

Also, each player will learn how to become more effective and efficient as well as how to deal with slumps and pressure situations. And you will get more enjoyment watching them play as their new skills develop.

To receive an information package (that explains some of the specialized drills I use) and to find out more about one-on-one training, please call my voice mail, or shoot me an email.

Voice Mail: ▓▓▓▓▓▓▓
Email: ▓▓▓▓▓▓▓▓▓▓▓▓▓.com

Please include *your name and address* in your message and the *age of each player.* I'll send your information package to you immediately. (Your personal information is safe, and I will never share it with anyone else in any way.)

Thank you,

Bill Dale

P.S. Because I only work with one player per hour, spots are limited and are filled on a first-come, first-served basis. To find out more about basketball lessons in the Elkton, Maryland and Newark, Delaware areas, please call or email right now to get your information package.

"Bill...You have done a great job with communicating the different skills in the game of basketball. Morgan Wootten said, '*This is the bottom line: Are we doing all we can to make our players' sports experience as rewarding as possible?*' It is programs like yours that can help our players grow even more! We count it a privilege to work with you and your program. In the future I will encourage my girls to come to your programs..."

— ▓▓▓▓▓▓▓▓▓, ▓▓▓▓▓▓▓ ▓▓▓▓▓▓▓, ▓▓▓▓▓ ▓▓▓▓▓▓▓▓ ▓▓▓▓▓▓▓

19

Flyer:

On the next 2 pages are copies of my flyers.

I gave this to parents as part of my referral system (that I talked about starting at the bottom of pg. 9).

I got permission to have a stack of these on a display table at a local high school tournament, and you should try to do the same thing.

You can also try to get them handed out at camps (especially if you volunteer to work at camps – and you <u>should</u> volunteer so you can get more exposure and practice training athletes).

One-on-One Basketball Training

<u>Private one-on-one training sessions</u> are available for:

- **beginners** who want help with the fundamentals,

- **players who have some experience** and are looking to get to the next level,

- and **experienced players** who want that extra "edge" over the competition.

With a focus on:	Helps develop higher levels of:
◆ Shooting ◆ Passing ◆ Dribbling ◆ Offensive Moves ◆ The "Mental Game"	◆ Accuracy ◆ Consistency ◆ Concentration ◆ Confidence

Each player gets:

1. Weekly **one-on-one training** sessions

2. **Customized training to fit their game** *(all players are different, so the training will be "made to fit" each player),*

3. A **Notebook** of print-outs, special shooting drills and tips for improving the mental aspects of shooting,

4. **Video Analysis** of their training *(players will be able to watch themselves doing the drills and using correct form in regular speed and in slow motion – <u>this reinforces what they learn</u>).*

Rates:

Single Lesson…………………………………...…..$45

Continuing Lessons………………………...………..$35 per lesson

"Bill…You have done a great job with communicating the different skills in the game of basketball. It is programs like yours that can help our players grow even more! We count it a privilege to work with you. In the future I will encourage my players to come to your programs..."

- ▬▬▬▬▬▬▬, ▬▬▬▬▬ ▬▬▬▬▬, ▬▬▬▬ ▬▬▬▬▬▬ **Academy**

For more information or to schedule training, please call Bill Dale at ▬▬▬▬▬▬▬▬
(please leave a message and let him know the best time for him to return your call).

*Spots are limited and are filled on a first-come, first-served basis.

Basketball Lessons (Shooting & Ball Handling)

Helps develop higher levels of <u>Accuracy</u>, <u>Consistency</u>, and <u>Concentration</u>, and leads to *more confidence*, *assertiveness*, and *more fun*.

The player who has more skills gets to spend more time on the court (more playing time)

<u>Who this is for:</u>

Players with little or some experience – Getting to the next level where a player can consistently make shots and also feel comfortable with dribbling and passing requires not only practicing, but practicing the right things. There are ways to leap over the "improvement wall" to get to that next level and increase confidence and consistency.

Experienced players – Even good players go through cold shooting streaks every now and then. But it's good to know how to get the "shooter's touch" and get into "the zone" as fast as possible. Also, when a good shooter increases accuracy and concentration – even just a little bit – it can have an enormous impact on shooting. And a good shooter who can also pass the ball becomes a valuable weapon on the court. This could be the "edge" that's needed to stand out above the competition.

Good Shooters Are *Made*, Not Born	Some Highlights of the Shooting Lessons:

All it takes is understanding and practicing all the little things that go into shooting. The drills we have are geared toward developing the 3 important parts of shooting:
    1. **Shooting Form**
    2. **Shooting Touch**
    3. **The "Mental Game"** (Concentration, Visualization, etc.)
All the basics will be covered, like: *shot release mechanics, developing a high arc, proper footwork, shooting off the dribble, offensive moves,* and *developing a consistent free throw routine,* etc.
	• The **perfect drill** that helps to develop **shooting form and touch**
	• How to properly warm up (*coming out onto the court to fire up 20-footers to warm up will throw off the mechanics of shooting faster than anything else*)
	• **9 practice drills** for becoming a better shooter from all over the court
	• 3 special drills to develop **concentration and focus** (successfully shooting a basketball requires high levels of focus and concentration)
	• Why using *mental movies* is important for **improving shooting**
	• How *self-talk* can lead to better shooting and **more confidence**
	• **Free throw routines** that'll help players focus on making the shots, instead of being worried about the crowd, the score, or what happens if they miss

Basketball Instructors: Bill Dale & _____

[Use this space for a picture, to talk about anybody (like an assistant) who is helping you do lessons, or to talk about something else you want to say about your business]

Dear parent or coach,

We wanted to let you know about our package of basketball lessons with **special drills and personal instruction** for developing all aspects of shooting and ball handling.

There's not enough room for me to explain everything here, but if you call me or shoot me an email, I'll mail you all the information about the lessons.

Please realize that **spots are very limited** and are filled on a first-come, first-served basis. Call or email for your information and enrollment forms today. (Lessons are available in Delaware and Maryland.)

Thank you for your interest,

Bill Dale
Phone: ███████████ (voice mail)
Email: ███████████████

"After Bill starting working with my daughter, her A.A.U. basketball coach mentioned that he noticed an improvement in her shooting."

For complete information, please call Bill Dale at ███████████ or email him at: ███████████████ (Please include your name, phone number, and address in your message.)

Business Card:

Here's a copy of one of my old business cards.

It's good to have some of these on hand, because you never know when you will run into someone who might be interested in lessons. As your word-of-mouth gets going, people will come up to you to talk and you should have a card ready for them.

There are a lot of different places to get business cards for very little money. Just do a search in Google. Some sites I found are listed in the Resources Section at the back of this manual.

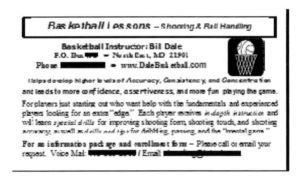

Special Events or Contests:

This is not only a great way to get students and players to sign up with you in your training business, it's also a great way to develop a following in your community.

I developed this when I had the idea to do something for the school that let me rent their gym for my training. I decided to put together a free throw contest for all of their players (and any other student who wanted to participate).

You can announce this on your Facebook page and on Instagram as well as your other social media. You can make a short video or simply a brief post telling all about it. Just make sure you give them all the info so they'll know what's going to be involved.

The coaches at the school had no problem helping me out, and you'll need some people to help you and make sure things go smoothly depending on what kind of event or contest you have for your sport.

You can get trophies, but I like to use medals from the Crown Trophy Company (CrownTrophy.com). It cost me around $100 (for all the medals) to put on this contest, but I saw it as an investment. Here's why - if you get just 1 or 2 students from this, you'll make that up, plus some. (And to tell you the truth, even if I didn't get any students from something like this, I'd still do it anyway. I like to "take care" of the school who allows me to rent their gym, so I want to do what I can for them and their students).

You can basically get the idea of what I did for this contest by looking at the next couple of pages. But let me again say that you can use this as a way to get more students. One thing to do is pass out the flyer for lessons that I just showed you back on pgs. 21-22 to parents who bring their kids to the contest.

As far as advertising the contest or event, you can pass out flyers for your event or contest (similar to the ways you pass out your regular lessons flyer, like at tournaments and camps) and run an ad in the newspaper, or make a post on Facebook and your website. (NOTE: Some local newspapers have a "What's Happening" area in the sports section where they print events for free. Check to see if your local paper does this so you can announce your contest or event for no cost).

2nd Annual **Free Throw Contest**

When: Saturday, March 12, 2005 at 1:30 pm
Where: ▮▮▮▮▮ School
Cost: Free
Deadline To Register: Saturday, March 5, 2005

There will be 2 divisions (Boys & Girls) and 3 age groups: 10-12; 13-15; 16-18. The top three scorers in each age group of each division will receive medals (First, Second, and Third Place). A total of 18 medals will be awarded.

To register players, please call Bill Dale at ▮▮▮▮▮ or email him at ▮▮▮▮▮com. Contest rules, more information, and results and photos from the 2004 Contest are available at www.▮▮▮▮▮.com

2nd Annual
Free Throw Contest

at Elkton Christian School

Sat. March 12, 2005
Starting at 1:30 P.M.

For Players Age 10 – 18

***Each player *must be* signed up by <u>March 5 , 2005</u>

---

2 Divisions:

Boys & Girls

3 Age Groups in each Division:

10-12 Years Old
13-15 Years Old
16-18 Years Old

The **top 3 scorers** in each age group in each division will receive medals
(First Place, Second Place, Third Place – a total of 18 medals will be awarded).

All players will get a basketball pin for participating and will be entered in a drawing for a new indoor / outdoor basketball.

Cost:

FREE

How To Register:

1. Please call Bill Dale at ▮▮▮▮▮▮▮▮▮▮ and leave a message on his voice mail with the name and age of each participant.
2. Or send him an email at ▮▮▮▮▮▮▮▮▮▮▮. In your email, please include your name and the name(s) and age(s) of your kid(s).

(Your personal information is safe and will not be rented, sold, or shared with anyone else).

***Each player *must be registered by <u>March 5, 2005</u>* so we can properly schedule the day's competition.

Please see other side of this flyer for a sample score card and contest rules.

Last year's results and photos are at:
www.FreeThrowContest.com

25

_____   _____

NAME   **AGE**

_____

BOY / GIRL

Official Use Only

◯ ◯ ◯ ◯ ◯ ◯ ◯ ◯ ◯ ◯ ◯ ◯ ◯ ◯ ◯

M = Make

X = Miss

The first made shot is worth one point, and each successful shot after a make is worth two points. After a miss, the next make is worth one point, etc. The highest possible score (15 consecutive made shots) is 29 points (1 one-pointer and 14 two-pointers).

SCORE: _____

Most Shots Made in a Row: _____
(For Tie-breaker)

Rules:

Each player will get 3 warm-up shots before their 15 official free throws are taken.

The first made shot is worth one point, and each successful shot after a make is worth two points. After a miss, the next make is worth one point, etc. The highest possible score (15 consecutive made shots) is 29 points (1 one-pointer and 14 two-pointers). (*This scoring system rewards players who can make a string of shots in a row. It also prevents a situation of endless tie-breaking "playoffs"*).

Tie-breakers: In the event that two or more players are tied with a high score, the player with the most shots made in a row will be awarded the win. If there are 2 or more players who are still tied after that, then there will be sudden death "shoot-off" rounds where each remaining player will take turns shooting one free throw. The winner of the sudden death "shoot-off" rounds will be the one who makes a shot while the others miss in the same round. Players who miss their shot in these "shoot-off" rounds are eliminated until only one player is left. If *all* of the players miss their shots (or if they all make their shots), then another round will take place until there is a winner.

How To Do Lessons

The great thing about this business is that you can teach whatever you want for whatever sport that you coach.

In basketball, the focus could be a lot of different things, from dribbling and rebounding, to passing, but my main focus is on shooting. As you know, a lot of kids (even so-called "good players") have problems with shooting. So I focussed on that the most. With baseball, it could be pitching and/or hitting, or fielding. In soccer, being a better goalie. In tennis, how to serve better. You get the idea.

In a couple of pages, I'll show you a typical run-down of one of my lessons so you can get an idea of how to put together a typical lesson or an hour of training. But for now I'll explain some of the equipment I've used.

Equipment

Actually, you can start out with nothing more than very basic equipment. That's how I started. Over time, I was able to buy more basketballs, orange cones that I use for certain drills, and stuff like that. For whichever sport you coach, there are all kinds of places on the internet where you can get pretty much all the equipment you'll need. I put some links at the end of this manual in the Resources Section.

If you are fortunate enough to get all of this stuff to begin with, that's great. If you can't do it just yet, then you can start out with basic equipment and gradually take some money that you get from lessons, and re-invest it in more equipment.

As an example of one of the special balls I used, here's one that shows the rotation of a player's shot. I think it's still available from www.KBACoach.com. I used it to help players see how the placement of their hands on the ball and the motion of their arms affected their shooting (the black line gets really "wobbly" if there is a lot mechanically wrong with their shots). Here it is:

Anyway, on the special equipment sites that I list in the Resources Section, you can get a lot of specialized training equipment like this.

Use of Video

One of the most important things you can do in your training is to be able to show your players exactly what they are doing. The only way to do that is to record video of them.

When I started out doing lessons, we didn't have smart phones with cameras. So I had to have an actual video camera. Today it's a lot easier to record clips so you can show what your players are doing right, and what they are doing wrong.

The best thing about it is that almost every kid has a smart phone with a camera today, so ask each one to open up their video camera so you can record clips of them doing the drills and practicing the moves you are teaching them. Then they can review the clips on their phone later.

You should take clips from several different angles so they can get an overall view of how the correct techniques for what you are doing look like from all those angles.

For example, here are a couple of pics that show you how I explain basketball free throws and the importance of how to line up and follow through on the shot. These are only pics, but when I take video of free throws from behind a kid taking the shots (like shown in these pics), I describe how the player looks in their shooting compared to these...

"Think 'straight' with proper body alignment…"

"A slightly open stance (where your foot and your hip on your shooting side are slightly angled, but not perfectly straight, toward the rim) allows everything to naturally line up...your shooting foot (where your toe is on the center of the free throw line), the ball, and the rim are in a perfect line. This will give you a better chance to send the ball in a straight line toward the basket. You'll also be able to see this better because your head (and eyes) will be in a more lined-up position for your shot. Free throws will be much easier when you get this down, because then it'll just be a matter of getting the right distance on your shots. And as you know, the distance is always the same on a free throw, so once you get your shooting mechanics and your rhythm down, you'll rarely miss to the left or right."

"All you are doing is sending the ball on a straight line, with the same arc, with the same distance, on each free throw."

30

It's good to take several clips of whatever you are having them do, then stop and have them look at the videos as you explain what they are doing right and how they can improve. You can erase most of them, but save a few so they can have them to review.

It's important that they have clips of them doing the techniques you are teaching them the correct way, so they can keep watching them and burning those into their memory. If a player doesn't have a camera phone, use yours, or a small video camera, so you can send the parents the clips so they can give them to their kid.

Actual Lessons

On pg. 30 is a copy of one of my typical lessons. Again, for whichever sport you teach, you'll have specific things you can do. So just go over mine and then you can get an idea of how to apply that to your sport.

If my lesson looks simple, that's because it is. You really don't need a lot of different things to do. Once you and your players get going, you'll see what each kid needs and you can spend however long you need on certain things.

Each player will be different, so you'll have to adapt to each one. But when you start out, you can have a general set of drills that you can use for everyone. Then you can pinpoint what each player needs and move on accordingly.

There are a lot of great DVD's and books with lots of drills for each sport on Amazon. There are also a lot of different Facebook Groups of coaches who share drills and training info. Just search for them the next time you are on Facebook. Or search YouTube for some drills or ideas.

Like I said before, you can do general all-around skill development, or focus on a couple aspects of your sport, like I did with basketball shooting and ball handling. It's up to you – it's *your* business.

I like to do 50 to 55 minute lessons (one lesson per week for each player). It's good for you to do less than an hour, especially if you have several in a row. This gives you a little time to get set up and ready for the next student, as well as rest for a few moments and get a drink.

I've seen where other coaches do one hour or even 45-minute lessons. It's all up to your preferences and how much time you get at the field or gym you use. I also like to set my lessons up in time "blocks" so I go to the gym for a few hours to do the lessons all in a row (all back-to-back). If you can do this, it's better than going back and forth to the field or the gym.

Again, I like to do one player at a time, but I have also done 2 or 3 at a time. Whatever you do, just be sure to plan out your lessons so you can get done what you want (and what the players need to work on). As you get used to doing this, the time starts to fly by. An hour goes by pretty quickly.

One other thing – I like to give them breaks whenever they need a drink. This is important if you are in a hot area. You don't want a player getting sick or fatigued. Tell them to bring bottled water with them so they have it ready and can get to it quickly when they are thirsty.

Used in my basketball lessons business...

Sample Lesson (55-minute lesson)
1:00pm – 1:55pm

1:00 – 1:15 pm --- Shooting Warm-ups
1. Floor Shooting Drill
2. Warm-up Drill
3. Catch and Pivot Drill
4. Dribble and Pivot Drill

1:15 – 1:25 pm --- Free Throw Shooting
-   I like to do sets of 2 or 3 shots and then have them back off the line (like in a game)

-   This is where I also use video to record their shots so they can see what they are doing

1:25 – 1:35pm --- Dribbling Drills

1:35 – 1:45pm --- Around-the-court Shooting Drills
-   This is where you can focus on different needs of each of your players. Guards and wing Forwards will spend more time with outside shots, and big Forwards and Centers underneath.

1:45 – 1:55pm --- Free Throw Shooting
-   Because I focus on shooting, I like to end with more free throws. You just can't get enough practice of free throws. It's good to do this at the end so you can help them with their free throw shooting when they are a little tired (like in a game).

* Also, if there is enough time, I'll have the player take shots around the court as I take stats for makes and misses at each spot.

During these lessons, when doing my specialized game-situation drills, I'll have the player go at "warm-up" speed. And gradually we'll go faster until the player is at game speed. They must ultimately get used to doing things at game speed ("practice how you'll play in a real game").

It's important to go slow if you are working with a young player so they understand what you are teaching them. Sometimes I'll even make a player walk through what I want them to do really slowly.

I'll do this for a couple of minutes. This has really helped a lot of the players, especially when they are learning something new or something that requires precision footwork.

Then we'll go a little faster, then work at it until they are at game speed. This could take a whole lesson, or it could take a couple of lessons before they make progress at the new skill.

I don't care how long it takes for a player to do something the right way. The most important thing is...We do not go forward until they do it the right way. That is your overall objective and purpose – to get players to play the right way fundamentally.

If I'm working with more than one player, I'll have each one take turns with some of the drills. I'll focus on the offensive player so I can make sure he or she is doing whatever we're working on the right way. And the other player will play defense – at first, light "shadow" defense, and gradually up to game-like defense.

After each lesson, I go over what I saw and I might give them "homework" – stuff they should work on so we can go over it next week. For instance, I might have them work on the footsteps of the new move we just worked on, or I might have them dribble only with their opposite hand until the next lesson. You'll be able to tell if they've done their homework. Most do, because they are there to get better.

After each lesson, before they leave, the parent will pay me (if they haven't paid upfront for a package of lessons) and I'll thank them and tell them I'll see them next week. Then get ready for the next session with the next student.

So that's how this kind of business works.

Again, the hardest part is probably going to be finding a stable place you'll be able to do your training sessions. And you might have to have a couple or a few locations if one place gets crowded. Just look at pgs. 4 and 5 again for my suggestions for that.

Once you find a place and do it for awhile it gets easier to organize. And like I said earlier, it's fun to be able to help kids get better at something they want to be good at.

Thank You and Good Luck

Thanks for investing in this information. This is a great business to be in and it's fun to be able to get a little money to help players become better.

One-on-one and small group sports training just keeps growing in popularity for players who are looking to get better at their sport. Players who love to play are looking for help to learn the fundamentals or to get an extra "edge" over other players. And parents are eager to pay someone for this kind of service for their children.

That someone is <u>You</u>.

If you have any questions or suggestions for me, just let me know.

Thanks again,

Bill

My Contact Info:

Bill Dale
Phone: 302-751-0045
Email: SportsCoachBiz@gmail.com

Resources

These are sites I have come across that I think will be a big help for you. I do not receive money for mentioning these. Do a little bit of research on each one and use what you think will be helpful to you.

Websites:
So people can find your business info and schedule training

www.CoachUp.com
www.SquareSpace.com
www.Wix.com
www.Weebly.com

Training Equipment:

www.SKLZ.com
www.AnthemSports.com
www.KBACoach.com
www.PerformBetter.com
www.Amazon.com (search for your sport, and training equipment)

Training Manuals / DVD's / Videos:

Amazon.com
YouTube.com (just search for drills for your sport)

Facebook Coaching Groups:

Facebook.com/PositiveCoachUS/ (Positive Coaching Alliance)
*Do a search on Facebook for other coaching and training pages for your sport

For Business Cards:

VistaPrint.com
Moo.com
GotPrint.com

For More Information About Starting A Sports Training Business:

SportsCoachBusiness.com

Free Bonus material:

To get the Bonus material that goes along with this book for using with your sports training business, please go to:

SportsCoachBusiness.com/bonus

Printed in Great Britain
by Amazon